20 LESSONS

=== THAT ===

BUILD A MAN'S
FITNESS

20 LESSONS
THAT
BUILD A MAN'S
FITNESS

A CONVERSATIONAL MENTORING GUIDE

VINCE MILLER

EQUIP PRESS

Colorado Springs

20 LESSONS
THAT
BUILD A MAN'S
FITNESS

Published by Equip Press, Colorado Springs, CO

First Edition: 2020
20 Lessons That Build A Man's Fitness / Vince Miller
Paperback ISBN: 978-1-951304-34-8
eBook ISBN: 978-1-951304-35-5

EQUIP PRESS

Colorado Springs

TO: _____

FROM: _____

NOTE: _____

_____

_____

_____

_____

_____

_____

_____

_____

_____

_____

_____

_____

CONTENTS

A NOTE FROM THE AUTHOR

Fitness is important to men. Well, most men. It's probably one of the easier conversations to strike up with another man. We will talk about pumping iron, getting yoked, our latest competition, or a current sports drama. Yet we fail to see the critical connecting points between fitness and our faith. And we shouldn't miss the connection. Paul didn't. Jesus didn't. We shouldn't. Those connections may be moments that could increase our understanding of faith and friendship while engaging in needed discipline and discussing biblically based principles with other men.

My hope for you is that these lessons give you something to discuss with a friend, relative, coworker, or even your children. I hope they will stir a discussion that will give you an opportunity to be proactive in your friendships and to pass on wisdom. May this mentoring relationship guide lead to greater success as you lead your business, team, non-profit, church, or your own family.

Let me encourage you to become part of a mentorship movement, either to mentor or be mentored.

Keep moving forward,

Live all in,

HOW TO USE TWENTY LESSONS THAT BUILD A MAN'S FITNESS

The Purpose

This 20-lesson guide is for mentors to use in private reflection or conversations with others. It's written to encourage conversations about leadership and character development among people of any age. It can be used repeatedly.

The Process

First, build yourself

Each time you read through a lesson, ponder privately on the reflection questions within the lesson. These lessons use the B.U.I.L.D. process:

- BEGIN with the goal.
- UNPACK your thoughts.
- INFORM through the Bible.
- LAND on action steps.
- DO one action for one week.

Second, partner up

Take each lesson further by partnering up with someone else. Use the 20 lessons as a mentoring tool that takes all the guesswork out of a leadership development conversation. Partner up with a friend, relative, co-worker, or someone in your family.

The Payoff

If you stay with the process for all 20 lessons you will grow in character, in your leadership, and in community with others. Often, we just need a plan to get moving. This book provides that plana method and a process resulting in outcomes with a rich payoff.

SPEAKER & AUTHOR VINCE MILLER

Abandoned at the age of two by his drug-using father, Vince Miller grew up in a challenging and anxiety-producing environment. He endured the strain of his mother's two failed marriages as well as her own drug use and poor choices. Fortunately, during Vince's formative teen years his grandfather, a man of faith, stepped up to mentor Vince, guiding him through a particularly difficult period.

Though he resisted initially, at the age of 20 Vince became a follower of Christ. Soon after, he would be at his grandfather's deathbed when cancer took his life. At that time Vince committed before God to "give back" by mentoring men as his grandfather had mentored him. Vince's story demonstrates the importance of mentors to support others in overcoming the enormous hurdles that manhood, mentoring, fathering, and leadership present to a man who wants to live in faith and character.

Audiences respond to Vince's stories. His teaching motivates, convicts, and sometimes even shocks the listener. Through stories of choices he made as a man, husband, father, and leader, Vince inspires men to lead and mentor others with an intelligent argument for faith.

After serving in notable organizations for more than 25 years (including Young Life, InterVarsity, and TCU Football), Vince founded *Resolute*, a non-profit organization focused on providing men with tools for mentorship. He's written numerous books and Bible study handbooks, along with producing small group videos that are resources for mentorship. His website, vincemiller.com, contains a Men's Daily Devotional read by thousands daily.

If you are looking for a motivational and engaging communicator for your next retreat, conference, or event, contact Vince Miller directly: www.vincemiller.com

Present Your Bodies

The human body has two ends on it:
one to create with and one to sit on.
Sometimes people get their ends reversed.
When this happens, they need a kick
in the seat of the pants.

THEODORE ROOSEVELT

If ever there was abundant evidence of an intelligent Creator and a Designer, it is in the human body. Have you ever given much thought to the beauty of the body's complexity? It's almost inexplicable: your heart beats more than 115,000 times a day, pumping life-sustaining blood to every cell of this mean machine we inhabit here on earth! It's a gift from God, for sure. But the body's real power is not just in any physical strength it might possess. Instead, it's in the way we employ our bodies in worship. Listen to what Paul says in Romans 12:1:

> *"I appeal to you, therefore, brothers, by the mercies of God, to present your bodies as a living sacrifice, holy and acceptable to God, which is your spiritual worship."*

Romans 12:1

One | The presented body

This power-packed verse is among one of the very first Bible verses that I recommend new believers to memorize. And with good reason: the Old Testament law required a guy to repeatedly present for the best of his best, a bull, goat, lamb, or dove as a sacrifice, to be absolved of his sins and be in right standing with God. But when JesusGod's Soncame along and died on the cross as the ultimate sacrifice for our sins, He fulfilled that requirement once and for all. The apostle Paul, writing to the believers in Rome, uses that ritual of sacrifice as a picture of what our response to God's free gift of grace should look like. Every day we should present ourselves, our minds and bodies, to God. *"I'm yours,"* we pray. *"God, I am so grateful for your gift of grace, and this is one way I can give back to you."*

Two | The living sacrifice

"Living sacrifice" is the ultimate oxymoron. *"Sacrifice"* implies death. So how can anything be a *"living sacrifice"*? The answer is pretty straightforward. We serve as living sacrifices whenever we give up our time and direct our activity toward serving the Lord. Take a moment and brainstorm a list of all the ways you might serve God.

Here are a few ideas to get you started:

- Help a neighbor with a project.
- Take a meal to a struggling friend.
- Mentor your son using the scripture.
- Join other believers in corporate worship through song.
- Carve out time each day to read and ponder God's Word.
- Dedicate some vacation time to serve on a mission trip.
- Take a friend to lunch and ask them if you can pray for something in their life.
- Tell the story of how you came to know Christ and the difference he has made in your life.

- Assess your skills and talents and find ways to use them for God's glory. For example, do you love cabinetry? Build a bookcase for a brother. Are you handy at plumbing? Fix that leak in the church kitchen. Do you enjoy hiking? Lead a group of kids on a weekend retreat.

You get the idea. We can serve God with our hands, our bodies, our mouths, our brainsthe list of possible *how-to's* is endless. The point is that we intentionallyevery daysacrifice our ***time*** and ***effort*** **in** ways that serve others and build God's kingdom.

Three | The holy and acceptable offering

This is a matter of stewardship. God has given us our bodies and our minds; the ball is in our court to take care of them as best we can. In this fallen world, we are, of course, subject to all manner of frailties and imperfections. But with a little imagination and creativity even our weaknesses can be employed to glorify God. But be aware: it's not enough just to take care of ourselves physically. We also must nurture and care for our hearts and minds, too.

Philippians 4:8 states:

> *"Finally brothers, whatever is true, whatever is honorable, whatever is just, whatever is pure, whatever is lovely, whatever is commendable, if there is any excellence, if there is anything worthy of praise, think about these things."*
>
> Philippians 4:8

We are responsible for presenting our best selves to God. All of us. Our hands, feet, eyes, thoughts, actions: everything. And praise God that He has given us His Holy Spirit to empower us, guide us, strengthen us every step of the way.

Reflection & Mentorship

Begin

- Our bodies are something we must present to God continually. They are our living sacrifice; the offering God wants.

Unpack

- Do men tend to think of their bodies selfishly or sacrificially?
- What does it require of a man to think this way about his physical body?

Inform

"I appeal to you, therefore, brothers, by the mercies of God, to present your bodies as a living sacrifice, holy and acceptable to God, which is your spiritual worship."

Romans 12:1

- What does the word "worship" mean in your own words?
- Do you think of your body as "holy and acceptable"? Why? Why not?

Land

- What bodily sacrifice do you need to make today?
- What would be the positive outcome if you followed through on this?

Do

- Act on your sacrifice.
- Tell a friend or mentor how this sacrifice impacted you.

Intentional Effort

Never give in. Never give in. Never, never, never, never in
nothing, great or small, large or petty never give in, except to
convictions of honor and good sense.

WINSTON CHURCHILL

You've heard it before: aim at nothing, and you'll end up hitting nothing.

Anything we accomplish in life requires intentionality. We set goals for ourselves in our jobs, in our daily lives to determine a direction. We make to-do lists of what we think will be essential to complete them, and when we do, we feel a sense of gratification (and maybe pride) when we reach our goals. Why should our approach to spiritual goals be any different?

But to be intentional means we have to exercise a little discipline. Paul likens it to training as an athlete.

> *"So I do not run aimlessly; I do not box as one beating the air. But I discipline my body and keep it under control, lest after preaching to others I myself should be disqualified."*

1 Corinthians 9:26-27

One | We run with purpose

A lot of people, consciously or subconsciously, believe in a cause-and-effect dynamic for most everything. In other words, *"you get back what you put in"* an idea loosely based in the Law of Reciprocity, which in a nutshell states that *"whatever you put out into the universe will eventually find its way back to you."*

But this isn't our Christian worldviewnot at all. We hold that God alone controls the universe, the world, and everything in it. As imperfect beings, however, we do recognize that the way we live can result in negative consequences for ourselves and sometimes for others. But we are motivated by God's grace and directed by His Holy Spirit, knowing we should put effort into living our lives to fulfill His purpose and spread His good news of the Gospel, to give our *all*, a championship effort, to (as I like to say) live *all in."*

Look at what Paul wrote in a letter to the church at Colossae:

> *"And so, from the day we heard, we have not ceased to pray for you, asking that you may be filled with the knowledge of His will in all spiritual wisdom and understanding, so as to walk in a manner worthy of the Lord, fully pleasing to Him: bearing fruit in every good work and increasing in the knowledge of God; being strengthened with all power, according to His glorious might, for all endurance and patience with joy; giving thanks to the Father, who has qualified you to share in the inheritance of the saints in light. He has delivered us from the domain of darkness and transferred us to the kingdom of His beloved Son, in whom we have redemption, the forgiveness of sins."*

Colossians 1:9-14

Two | Discipline is needed

This means as *spiritual athletes in training* then, we must commit to disciplines that work in unison with the Holy Spirit. We cannot ignore the needed discipline. Read what Paul says:

"Do you not know that in a race all the runners run, but only one receives the prize? So run that you may obtain it."

1 Corinthians 9:24

As we know, old habits die hard, so it benefits us to work out every single day. We must build up our resistance to sin, develop the capacity to say *no*, and to improve the way we run with daily discipline. To the Romans Paul wrote:

"Let not sin therefore reign in your mortal body, to make you obey its passions. Do not present your members to sin as instruments for unrighteousness, but present yourselves to God as those who have been brought from death to life, and your members to God as instruments for righteousness. For sin will have no dominion over you, since you are not under law but under grace."

Romans 6:12-14

A word of warning: God's grace does not, of course, give us a license to sin! Notice what Paul also states:

"What then? Are we to sin because we are not under law but under grace? By no means! Do you not know that if you present yourselves to anyone as obedient slaves, you are slaves of the one whom you obey, either of sin, which leads to death, or of obedience, which leads to righteousness? But thanks be to God, that you who were once slaves of sin have become obedient from the heart to the standard of teaching to which you were committed, and, having been set free from sin, have become slaves of righteousness."

Romans 6:15-18

Discipline is needed as we run the spiritual race.

Three | Never disqualified

Our belief is founded in the grace God extends, evidenced by the effort we give. While our effort does not save us, it *is* evidence of our radical belief. It's only by the power of the Holy Spirit, however, that we can walk a Christlike walk. Still, it's a choice we must make every day: to keep turning our hearts (and bodies) to live according to God's promises.

> *"For this very reason, make every effort to supplement your faith with virtue, and virtue with knowledge, and knowledge with self-control, and self-control with steadfastness, and steadfastness with godliness, and godliness with brotherly affection, and brotherly affection with love. For if these qualities are yours and are increasing, they keep you from being ineffective or unfruitful in the knowledge of our Lord Jesus Christ."*

2 Peter 1:5-8

God sees our hearts and our desire to please Him, and even in our weakest moments He never gives up on us. So we must stand firm and never give up on ourselves. With the help of the Holy Spirit, we persevere, and like Paul, we are never disqualified.

Reflection & Discussion

Begin

- We must give intentional effort as we run the spiritual race. We need discipline.

Unpack

- Do Christians take God's grace for granted?
- What would it look like to abuse the grace of God?

Inform

"For this very reason, make every effort to supplement your faith with virtue, and virtue with knowledge, and knowledge with self-control, and self-control with steadfastness, and steadfastness with godliness, and godliness with brotherly affection, and brotherly affection with love. For if these qualities are yours and are increasing, they keep you from being ineffective or unfruitful in the knowledge of our Lord Jesus Christ."

2 Peter 1:5-8

- What do the words *"make every effort"* mean to you?
- How do we know when *"these qualities"* are *"increasing,"* as Peter says?

Land

- Is there a place in your spiritual life you are not giving effort, but should?

Do

- Tell a mentor or friend where you need to give specific spiritual effort.
- Act on this three times over the next seven days.

Your Temple

I still enjoy watching a batter successfully cross home plate,
but nothing thrills me more than seeing the Holy Spirit at work
in hearts as the Gospel is carried into stadiums, across the
airwaves, and around the world.

BILLY GRAHAM

Most of us live in some type of dwelling place: a house, an apartment, a trailer, a tent, or someplace we call home. If you're a fisherman, you might live on a boat. If you're a forest ranger, you might live in a cabin. If you're a king, you might live in a palace. But where does the Holy Spirit live? It's a lot closer than you think: the Holy Spirit lives in you. Did you get that? The Holy Spirit lives in *you*. Take a look at Paul's letter to the people in Corinth.

> *"Or do you not know that your body is a temple of the*
> *Holy Spirit within you, whom you have from God?*
> *You are not your own, for you were bought with a price.*
> *So glorify God in your body."*
>
> 1 Corinthians 6:19-20

One | The Spirit lives in you

Think about the roles God's Spirit performs in our lives. For one thing, He is our helper. He helps us in myriad ways:

> *"And I will ask the Father, and he will give you another Helper, to be with you forever, even the Spirit of truth, whom the world cannot receive, because it neither sees Him nor knows Him. You know Him, for He dwells with you and will be in you."*

John 14:16-17

> *"But the Helper, the Holy Spirit, whom the Father will send in my name, He will teach you all things and bring to your remembrance all that I have said to you."*

John 14:26

> *"Nevertheless, I tell you the truth: it is to your advantage that I go away, for if I do not go away, the Helper will not come to you. But if I go, I will send Him to you. And when He comes, He will convict the world concerning sin and righteousness and judgment."*

John 16:7-8

He gives us the power to be witnesses for Jesus:

> *"But you will receive power when the Holy Spirit has come upon you, and you will be my witnesses in Jerusalem and in all Judea and Samaria, and to the end of the earth."*

Acts 1:8

He strengthens us when we are weak:

> *"Likewise, the Spirit helps us in our weakness. For we do not know*
> *what to pray for as we ought, but the Spirit himself intercedes for*
> *us with groanings too deep for words. And He who searches hearts*
> *knows what is the mind of the Spirit, because the Spirit intercedes for*
> *the saints according to the will of God."*

Romans 8:26-27

The Holy Spirit is an incredible resource for us in many ways and on many levels. What better place is there for Him to reside than within us as believers? It's genius. We have total access to the greatest power in the universe: the limitless power of the Spirit. And that's by design. It's the way God wants it. Kind of blows your mind, doesn't it?

Two | Your body is now God's

Here's another mindbender: Paul says we are *"not our own."* God owns us. It's a good thing God is full of love, grace, mercy, and wisdom, because He owns us. We were bought and paid for by the blood of Jesus. He is our Savior, indeed, but He also is our Lord, our Master. When we misuse or abuse our bodies, we are messing with someone else's property, and that someone else just happens to be Creator and Ruler of the universe. Think about that the next time you're tempted to engage in an activity you know to be wrong in God's eyes. At the same time, however, don't forget that you have direct access to all the power you need to resist that temptation.

Three | Your body is for God's Glory

As much as we'd like to enjoy a little personal glory now and then, it's just no longer simply about us. We belong to God, so every accomplishment and accolade belongs to Him. There's nothing wrong with pursuing excellence,

27

doing marvelous things in excellent ways, but perspective is everything. What's our motive? Are we in it for the glory it brings to ourselves, or are we in it to bring glory to God?

When Solomon built the Temple of the Lord in Old Testament Israel he did so according to God's exacting standards and specifications. Gifted craftsmen used only the very finest timber, precious metals, and other materials to erect the magnificent structure. When it was completed, God said to Solomon:

> *"I have heard your prayer and your plea, which you have made before Me. I have consecrated this house that you have built, by putting My name there forever. My eyes and my heart will be there for all time."*

1 Kings 9:3

God has chosen your body (and my body) to be His holy temple. I admit that we may grow weary of what seems to us like frailties and imperfections in our bodies, but God has nonetheless chosen this earthly shell we inhabit as the dwelling place for His Holy Spirit. So with His help, let us strive every day to treat our bodies as the Temple of God, and live accordingly.

Reflection & Discussion

Begin

- We are a temple of the Spirit of God, owned and used by him for his purposes.

Unpack

- Do Christian men recognize that we are a temple of the Spirit?

- What needs to be done for us to come to terms with this reality?

Inform

"Or do you not know that your body is a temple of the Holy Spirit within you, whom you have from God? You are not your own, for you were bought with a price. So glorify God in your body."

1 Corinthians 6:19-20

- Why do you think the Corinthians had forgotten that their bodies were a *"temple of the Holy Spirit"*?
- What are the consequences of being "owned" by God?
- You were "bought for a price," so what was the price?

Land

- Since God sees value in purchasing you, how should you see your worth?
- What value do you bring in your present body to the kingdom?
- How can you live this out today?

Do

- Act on this with immediacy, today.

The Race

"I always loved running . . . it was something you could do
by yourself, and under your own power. You could go in any
direction, fast or slow as you wanted, fighting the wind if you
felt like it, seeking out new sights just on the strength of your
feet and the courage of your lungs."

JESSE OWENS

"Do you not know that in a race all the runners run, but only
one receives the prize? So run that you may obtain it. Every
athlete exercises self-control in all things. They do it to receive
a perishable wreath, but we an imperishable. So I do not run
aimlessly; I do not box as one beating the air."

1 CORINTHIANS 9:24-26

love how Paul combines the spiritual life and the spiritual race as he
communicates the importance of discipline to the Corinthian church. His
comparison is obvious, but how do we do it?

One | Get A Goal

Few athletes would train for or compete in a race if there's no goal at the
endno prize for winning. In this letter to the Corinthians Paul encourages

believers to run the race so that we may obtain not a perishable prize, but an imperishable one. Back in his day, winners of races received wreaths (rather than brass trophies or cash purses) that would eventually wither and dry up. It's a great metaphor, but what is Paul really talking about? What was the imperishable prize he had in his sights? Consider the context. Just a few lines earlier in his letter, Paul writes:

"What then is my reward? That in my preaching I may present the gospel free of charge..."

1 Corinthians 9:18

He goes on to write:

"I have become all things to all people, that by all means I might save some. I do it all for the sake of the gospel, that I may share with them in its blessings."

1 Corinthians 9:22-23

So yes: we train and discipline ourselves to grow in righteousness and in our relationship with God, but beyond that, Paul's ultimate aim is to spread the gospel and win people for Christ.

Two | Get Self-Control

"Every athlete exercises self-control in all things," Paul writes. His comparison to an athlete training for and competing in a race continues. The athlete consumes a healthy diet. And we, as Christian men, nurture our hearts and minds with God's Word. The athlete works out physically. We meditate on Scripture and drop to our knees in prayer. The athlete maintains sharp mental focus. That means we focus on the Lord in everything we do. The athlete makes personal sacrifices to keep his eyes on the prize. Paul writes in

1 Corinthians 9 that he sacrifices his rights as an apostle to eliminate *"any obstacle in the way of the gospel of Christ"* (1 Corinthians 9:12).

What are you willing to sacrifice for the sake of the gospel? Where do you need to get self-control?

> *"But I discipline my body and keep it under control, lest after preaching to others I myself should be disqualified."*
>
> 1 Corinthians 9:27

Three | Get Perseverance

None of this is easy. Athletes train for a race and run with dogged determination. We, too, must be doggedly persistent. We must persevere. Our spiritual muscles may burn, but do we quit? Nope. Instead, we lean in. We don't give up. We pace ourselves. Among our most significant challenges along the way, perhaps, will be to achieve a healthy balance in our lives. Think about your typical week. If you're like a lot of guys, you work a minimum of 40 hours a week, you commute to your job, you run errands, you tend to a few chores around the house, you spend time with your family, you eat, and, oh yeah: occasionally you sleep. How do you squeeze in any spiritual discipline?

I have two words for you: **intentionality** and **planning**.

But don't forget that as believers, as brothers in Christ, we have the best cheering section ever,better than any athlete's biggest fans. We have the Lord. Like Paul says:

> *"I can do all things through Him who strengthens me."*
>
> Philippians 4:13

Amen to that, brother!

Reflection & Mentorship

Begin

- We are called to run a spiritual race by getting a goal, self-control, and perseverance.

Unpack

- How is your stamina in the spiritual race right now? Are you energized or depleted? Why is this so?
- Which of the three points above stood out to you?

Inform

"Do you not know that in a race all the runners run, but only one receives the prize? So run that you may obtain it. Every athlete exercises self-control in all things. They do it to receive a perishable wreath, but we an imperishable. So I do not run aimlessly; I do not box as one beating the air."

1 Corinthians 9:24-26

- What does it look like to *"run that you may obtain it"*?
- What does *"self-control"* look like for a runner? Consider what a runner must eliminate, and also act upon.
- What does it mean to *"not run aimlessly,"* and why did Paul add this in with this metaphor?

Land

- Where are you running aimlessly?
- What act of self-control would help you right now?

Do

- Pray for one week about your need for self-control.
- Then run with purpose by exerting one act of self-control for the week.

The Need for Rest

"I have the habit of attention to such excess, that my senses get no rest but suffer from a constant strain."

HENRY DAVID THOREAU

"And he said, 'My presence will go with you, and I will give you rest.'"

EXODUS 33:14

Fitness experts tell us that regimens of physical training with no built-in breathers can counteract an athlete's hard work. Too little rest can make a man crabby; render him more susceptible to injury; induce adrenal fatigue, thereby increasing the production of the fat-storing hormone cortisol; hamper his sleep cycle (which then introduces another whole set of health problems); compromise his immune system; and mess with his performance level (and I don't mean just on the track, court, or playing field). Our efforts to serve God well and grow spiritually also must be punctuated by periods of rest. I'm not advocating laziness, but I also do not suggest that we emulate the guy who never sits down. Too often, we worship the god of activity rather than the God who gives us rest. In short, there are times in life that call for a little self-care.

One | You may need rest

Do not (and I repeat: *do not*) wait to rest until you begin to observe the tell-tale signs that you need it. By then, you're overdue. I'm talking about things like physical fatigue, loss of passion for spiritual activity, feeling far from God, lack of the desire to serve—you get the picture. Indeed, when we are ambushed by a symptom or two, we should not hesitate to step back for a bit. But even better, we ought to anticipate our need for rest and make it a regular part of our routine. We do so at the invitation of Jesus Himself, as quoted in Matthew's gospel:

> *"Come to me, all who labor and are heavy laden,*
> *and I will give you rest."*

> Matthew 11:28

Two | You may need relaxation

Meditation on God's Word is good for us all. Picture yourself stretched out on a poolside lounge relaxing with a good book. Why not make it *The Good Book?*

Any time we find a quiet place of solitude to lose ourselves in Scripture it is incredibly refreshing. We hear a lot about having a daily *"quiet time"* with God, and some of us have made that a habit, but just because it's become a bit of a cliché in Christian circles doesn't mean it should be dismissed out of hand. I highly recommend it. It's cliché because it works!

But there are myriad other worthwhile ways to relax as well. Putter in the garage, engage in a hobby, play a video game, doze on the couch—take a little time and do it. You may be so busy that you have to actually schedule it, but that's okay. Just make sure you don't neglect it.

Three | You may need recreation

Sometimes it is good just to play. And I do mean *play*.

There's some overlap with relaxation, but I think of playing as something that requires a different kind of energy. Board games or card games with friends or family are great, even if they do sort of straddle the fence between relaxing and playing. But sometimes playing helps us to disconnect from the pact and pattern of everyday life. If you're a dad, roughhouse with the kids. Play golf, or tennis, or softball. Go fishing or hiking. Take the family to a theme park or to the splash pad just around the corner. I bet you could brainstorm a list of 20 fun ways to play in about as many seconds.

Rest, relaxation, and recreation: all are forms of the kind of break from the routine we need for maximum physical, mental, emotional, and spiritual health. The fitness experts are right. Rest is biblical. And it's essential. God set a precedent:

> *"And on the seventh day God finished His work that He had done,*
> *and He rested on the seventh day from all His work that*
> *He had done."*

> Genesis 2:2

And Jesus encourages it:

> *"And He said to them (His disciples), 'Come away by yourselves to*
> *a desolate place and rest awhile.' For many were coming and going,*
> *and they had no leisure even to eat. And they went away in the boat*
> *to a desolate place by themselves."*

> Mark 6:31-32

What should be our response? Get some rest!

Reflection & Mentorship

Begin

- We all need times of rest, relaxation, and recreation: it's biblical.

Unpack

- Do you tend to be overwork, underwork, or do just the right amount of work?
- What do you do to replenish and restore?

Inform

> *"And He said to them (His disciples), 'Come away by yourselves to a desolate place and rest awhile.' For many were coming and going, and they had no leisure even to eat. And they went away in the boat to a desolate place by themselves."*

Mark 6:31-32

- What is good about a "desolate" place?
- Why does Jesus want his men to do this?
- What would be restoring about being on the boat for Jesus's closest disciples?

Land

- What kind of restoration do you need today?
- What action do you need to take?
- How can you take time to do this, this week?

Do

- Take the needed action, and report back how this felt to a friend, mentor, or loved one.

Training in Godliness

I hated every minute of training, but I said, "Don't quit. Suffer now and live the rest of your life as a champion."

MUHAMMAD ALI

"For while bodily training is of some value, godliness is of value in every way, as it holds promise for the present life and also for the life to come."

1 TIMOTHY 4:8

Can you imagine pushing through a 25-hour-per-week training regimen of swimming, biking, and running for an entire year with no particular goal in mind? Why would a guy do that? Most wouldn't, I'm guessing. But anyone serious about competing in the Ironman Triathlon just might. When the day of the big event arrives, you're facing a 2.4-mile swim, a 112-mile bike ride, and a marathon run of 26 miles and 385 yards. That's the goal: to compete, finish the race, and possibly even win. Only one person can win, of course, but even to just finish would yield a moment or two of personal accomplishment and glory. Indeed, physical training has its rewards. But (there's always a *"but"*) what about your heart, mind, and soul? What about the part of you that is eternal?

One | Right Comparisons in Training

"Bodily training is of some value," Paul writes to Timothy, "but godliness is of value in every way."

Don't get me wrong. I will always advocate taking good care of your physical body, practicing good health habits, eating right, and getting a decent amount of sleep and exercise. We come in assorted shapes and sizes and all manner of imperfection, but God calls us to be good stewards of everything He's given us, and that would include our "earth suits." After all, God's Holy Spirit dwells there.

"Or do you not know that your body is a temple of the Holy Spirit within you, whom you have from God? You are not your own, for you were bought with a price. So, glorify God in your body."

1 Corinthians 6:19-20

It's not that we should neglect our bodies to focus our attention exclusively on spiritual health and growth. It is, however, a matter of priorities. Take care of our bodies, yes, but even more, nurture our hearts and exercise our minds to know and love God better and better. The benefit is long-term. There is real eternal value in a spiritual investment.

Two | Right Balance in Training

There is, in the comparison, some implied extremism. Caring only for the body and not the spirit is to miss the point of the passage. To be a fitness fanatic is to turn fitness into a god and to miss the real thing, God Himself. But caring only for the spirit and not the body is reckless and irresponsible. True, there are physical maladies, frailties, and limitations we can't prevent or control. But it just makes sense that we can maximize our effectiveness for Christ when we pay proper attention to our physical health. So how does one strike the best balance between physical and spiritual training?

It's a matter of daily discipline. We must do both. And if we're really creative, we can combine the two. Pray while you jog. Dig into God's Word while you rest. Share the Gospel over a nutritious meal. You get the idea. This is entirely doable, guys.

Three | Right Priorities in Training

It is possible to overdo almost anything, of course, be it food, friends, finances, fitness, the list goes on. It's all about our priorities. But there is one thing that is absolutely impossible to overdo. And it's the key to everything. Here it isare you ready for this? The key to ensuring that our priorities are in order is our complete and total focus on God. Call it an obsession if you will. When we are meditating on God's Word or kneeling in prayer, He is our focus. And when our primary motive in going for a jog or lifting weights is the care and maintenance of God's temple, He is our focus. Why do we make it so hard when it really is as simple as that?

We train both physically and spiritually. Both are importantboth matter. If we err to one side or the other, let's err to the spiritual side. But through it all, let's keep the main thing the main thing. God must remain our focus. Period.

At the end of the race waits a forever paradise with the King of the universe. And the big win is not that we finish first. The big win is that we break that yellow tape arm in arm with as many fellow human beings as possible.

So ready, set, go! See you at the finish line.

Reflection & Mentorship

Begin

- Spiritual and physical training are both important, and we must make right comparisons, right balance, and right priorities as we train.

Unpack

- Do you feel you are giving an excellent balance to your physical and spiritual training? If not, where do you need to tip the scales?
- How does a lack of one or the other affect you?

Inform

"For while bodily training is of some value, godliness is of value in every way, as it holds promise for the present life and also for the life to come."

1 Timothy 4:8

- List the values of "some training" of the body.
- List how "godliness" is a value in "every way" for men.

Land

- What do you need to do physically?
- What do you need to do spiritually?

Do

- Take action by striking more balance this week.
- Do a workoutthe one you need.

Physical Stewardship

I think permitting the game to become too physical takes away a little bit of the beauty.

JOHN WOODEN

Today I think most would agree we worship sports and athletic accomplishments based on how much money we spend on the pursuit of these things. But it is fascinating because, amidst our attraction, many nevertheless miss seeing and understanding the value of bodily stewardship. We, by far, enjoy the drama, the competition, or discussion but sometimes fail to see the great life lessons in fitness, exercise, coaching, and athletic pursuit.

I wish that many years ago, when I was a teen and young adult that someone would have reinforced to me that I only get one body (a single physical machine) for an entire lifetime and that I must care for it for a lifetime. While we might think this is intuitive, my younger mind always thought I was invincible and unbreakable, and what I put into it and got out of it could be pushed to the limits every day without consequence. Yet this state of mind overlooks the importance of stewarding the physical machine we are given.

Here are a few essential thoughts on good physical stewardship.

One | Physical care is good stewardship

Now may the God of peace himself sanctify you completely, and may your whole spirit and soul and body be kept blameless at the coming of our Lord Jesus Christ.

1 Thessalonians 5:23

In this life, we are called to steward many things as men. One of the things we often default to thinking about is the stewardship of money. But there are a lot of other things we stewardone we often overlook is our body. The "machine" God gave to each of us during our lifetime is important. It serves an essential purpose, and we must steward it with care. This means we should understand physical care and exercise as needed, and not something we should neglect. We are only given one biological machine for carrying around our spirit and soul, and therefore, we must steward it with excellence. Notice Jesus's remarks in the Book of Luke:

One who is faithful in a very little is also faithful in much, and one who is dishonest in a very little is also dishonest in much. If then you have not been faithful in the unrighteous wealth, who will entrust to you the true riches? And if you have not been faithful in that which is another's, who will give you that which is your own?

Luke 16:10-12

The life principle is this: how we steward the small things, wealth, or otherwise mattersthis is true of anything, including the body. Our body is our means of human existence, interaction, witness, and communication with others. We feed it so that we can have the energy we need to be faithful and fulfill our responsibilities in living out the good news as a witness to the world. This machine needs quality inputs and outputs to ignite strength and vitality to do God's daily work. And it's our individual responsibility to care for it.

Two | God cares about your physical body

And Jesus stretched out his hand and touched him, saying, "I will; be clean." And immediately his leprosy was cleansed.

Matthew 8:3

If Jesus didn't care about our bodies, he would not have healed people. But he did so frequently and for many reasons. With renewed energy, men and women who were healed by Jesus went on their way, praising God and telling the world about the One who heals spiritual afflictions and physical ailments. These men and women went forward in life, walking again, seeing again, and experiencing community again. If they were hungry, Jesus fed them. If they were bleeding, Jesus touched them. If they were dying, Jesus saved them. Jesus did these things for people who wanted healed machines, and these people went forward, knowing that they should care for their bodies, stewarding them, because God values spirit and body.

Three | God cares primarily about your eternity

And when he saw their faith, he said [to the paralyzed man], "Man, your sins are forgiven you."

But that you may know that the Son of Man has authority on earth to forgive sins" — he said to the man who was paralyzed — "I say to you, rise, pick up your bed and go home."

Luke 5:20, 24

This instance is interesting. Jesus heals both the paralyzed man's spiritual and physical needs, but notice that Jesus addressed his spiritual needs first. Which if you read the story, you'll discover created an exciting moment of tension and controversy for a few religious leaders. But this is Jesus, always stirring up controversy by ordering things precisely and correctly.

The general principle is we discover from the order that Jesus performed this healing is "stewardship of the body," not the "worship of the body." We can overdo anything, including how we care and tend to the body. While caring for the machine we are given, we should be careful about giving our bodies, sports, or even athletic pursuits priority over Godto the point they become God. Our bodies are the means of worship, not what we worship. Our primary need is for a relationship with God through the forgiveness that God provides, which is why Jesus does this first in the case of this paralyzed man. And at this moment, Jesus puts a big punctuation mark on its importance by doing it first.

The lesson is this: steward with care what God has given to you. And steward it in such a way it gives glory to God, not yourself. The body God gave you is your means of witness to the greatness of God. Run this life with endurance and do so with the health and physical stamina God gave you and so run the race with endurance.

Reflection & Mentorship

Begin

- Our physical machines, our bodies, are the means of worship and witness of God.

Unpack

- Do we worship the body today? What evidence do you see for or against your conclusion?
- Do we worship athletic events? What evidence do you see for or against your conclusion?

Inform

And when he saw their faith, he said [to the paralyzed man],
"Man, your sins are forgiven you."

But that you may know that the Son of Man has authority on earth
to forgive sins" — he said to the man who was paralyzed — "I say to
you, rise, pick up your bed and go home."

Luke 5:20, 24

- Why does Jesus heal this paralyzed man?
- Why does he do this in this order?

Land

- Which of the three points stood out to you above? Why?
- What steps do you need to take today?

Do

- Take one action to address your physical body and steward it better this coming week.

The Fit Mind

It's no surprise that (regardless of our faith in God or not) many view God in numerous different ways. This has always been the case. Our view of the unseen God is often adversely affected by cultural and social experiences and lead to false assumptions about the invisible God. Therefore, some view God as distant, unengaged, authoritative, critical, or even harsh.

And note: how we view God in our mind, absolutely matters.

Consider for a moment what A.W. Tozer says:

> *"What comes into our minds when we think about God is the most important thing about us."*

His statement is spot on, and it's taken from one of his classic works, *Knowledge of the Holy*. In this book Tozer also says:

> *"For this reason, the gravest question before the church is always God himself. And the most portentous fact about any man is not what he at any given time may say or do, but what he and his deep heart conceives God to be like. We tend by a secret law of the soul to move toward our mental image of God."*

This means that keeping our mind fit, just like we strive to keep our body fit, is essential as it affects everything about us. The apostle Paul addressed this in Romans 12.

> *I appeal to you therefore, brothers, by the mercies of God, to present your bodies as a living sacrifice, holy and acceptable to God, which*

is your spiritual worship. Do not be conformed to this world, but be transformed by the renewal of your mind, that by testing you may discern what is the will of God, what is good and acceptable and perfect.

Romans 12:1-3

As every athlete addresses their physical conditioning, they cannot ignore how they think about their body in preparation, play, and performance. While getting started physically might be easy, we will all soon discover that fitness requires a keen mental capacity to stay engaged. We must have a mindset of willingness to overcome bad behaviors, defeating thoughts, and negative attitudes pushing the body to accomplish something that the body and mind consider unattainable. Similarly, every Christian must have a fit mind for how we think about God so that we can overcome bad behaviors, defeating thoughts, and negative attitudes. It's a daily mental workout.

So here are three mental activities that Paul suggests to be fit in mind.

One | We must live like we are dying.

"Present your bodies as a living sacrifice."

Paul uses two words in conjunction here that call to mind a powerful mental image of something we participate in spiritually. He's calling us to present our bodies as a "living sacrifice." These two words, in combination, are unusual because there would seem to be no such thing as a "living sacrifice." Sacrifices were offered dead, not living.

Paul is trying to connect past imagery to present activity. God has been teaching all humanity about sacrifice since the beginning of time, culminating in the sacrifice of Jesus. And with Jesus Christ, he has embossed on our minds the importance of sacrifice. Paul wants us to understand that we carry the same sacrificial system forward. But now it's not the presentations of dead sacrifices but living sacrifices. It's us living daily as the sacrifice. It's a sacrifice of bodily proportions. But we have to have a mind for this!

And how do we do this? Well, we live like we're dying. And yes, we are all physically dying all day long, but there is a deeper connection. We live like we are dying, not just physically, but like we are dying to self and selfish desires spiritually. This is why we no longer need a lamb, goat, bull, or bird. We are the sacrifice. And this sacrifice requires a mind that is aware of our sin and self-desires and presents them to God on a continual daily basis.

But who do we present this sacrifice to?

Two | We make daily sacrifices to God.

"Holy and acceptable to God, which is your spiritual worship."

It's easy to misunderstand spiritual worship. It's far more listening to music being played by guys on stage in skinny jeans. It's so much more. The daily sacrifices we offer takes us well beyond that. It's presenting what is unholy in us as a holy and acceptable sacrifice to God. I know this sounds like it's backward, but it is not. To offer our sin and sinful desires to God with a repentant heart is the most acceptable form of worship. It's the gym of Christpresenting our behaviors, thinking, and attitudes to God so that we can become more like Christ.

Three | We fight conformity to the world.

"Do not be conformed to this world, but be transformed by the renewal of your mind."

Do you feel the forming in these words? It's a form and shape change. Like a healthy diet and regular exercise form the body, so must the Christian be formed. But our forming comes from non-conforming. We are non-conforming to the world. But by what activity and in what gym? The answer is simple by lifting the weights of renewal in the gym of the mind.

As when we stay with the process that Paul presents, we will quickly discover that we have a lot to do in the gym of the mind. This requires awareness, stamina, willingness, accountability, and encouragement in the daily repetition. While we are familiar with the physical and tangible, the spiritual and abstract challenges of being fit in mind are a new exercise program for all of us. But as you stay with it, you will discover that God will become more evident, and life in his gym produces incredible results.

Reflection & Mentorship

Begin

- What comes to mind matters there we as men must stay fit in our minds?

Unpack

- Do you think about what your mind consumes? Why or why not?
- Have you ever thought about having a "fit" mind?
- What kinds of "exercises" are need to stay "fit" in your mind?

Inform

"Present your bodies as a living sacrifice."

Romans 12:1

- How do you now understand the phrase "living sacrifice"?
- Discuss how adopting this mindset would affect how you view all of life.

Land

- What do you need to do daily to stay "fit in mind?"
- What small steps do you need to take today?

Do

- Share one mental fitness activity you are going to start doing today.

The Essential Coach

Often, we see Jesus only see Jesus as a teacher, and therefore we miss some of the great coaching he did. Jesus was not only an educator, but he knew how to coach men. As men, husbands, fathers, and leaders, we will have to be coaches in many instances. Coaching is not just for venues like sports and life-improvement. Every man will have to coach in some area of his life. The people who have tested my coaching ability the most have been my children and second my employees. Some of this is due to me and my ability and inability, and some of this is due to them and their ability and inability. But I have come to learn that, notably as a father and leader, I am going to be coaching a lot through life; therefore, understanding some essential skills in how Jesus did it would be valuable if not crucial.

A Coach Asks

[Jesus] answered them, "What did Moses command you?"

Mark 10:3

If you read through Jesus's life and interactions, you will discover he ask a lot of questions. He asked more questions than he gave answers. After counting, one will find that Jesus asked over 300 questions, and he only answers about half of them. This was common practice for Jesus and teachers in his day.

Great spiritual coaches stimulate the thinking of others to drive them toward truth. Yes, he could have just given them the answers, but Jesus loved to ask questions for one reasonto expose the motivation of a man's heart.

As a coach, we have to do the same. Sometimes, we need to tell certain moments will dictate this, but sometimes we need to ask. Asking is not quick, requires effort and forethought, and requires the other person to reflect and respond for themselves. This is not just developing the practice of critical thinking; it's helping others to see the motivations behind their thoughts and behaviors and driving for spiritual change. When we do this, we use spiritual questions and help drive for deeper and more permanent change.

Just consider the question above. In this interchange, a group of religious lawyers were trying to trap Jesus. Jesus, knowing their motivation, returns their question with a question, and then, therefore, rather than just giving the best answer, exposed them before a crowd of people. Essentially, he said, "What does the Bible say?" And in doing so, Jesus avoids what could be a public predicament, and uses it to both expose their motivation but also drive them toward spiritual and scriptural truth. And we should do the same. The craft does not come easily, but we will never be done coaching, and it begins not just with having great answers but with asking better questions.

A Coach Affirms

> *He said to him the third time, "Simon, son of John, do you love me?"*
> *Peter was grieved because he said to him the third time, "Do you love*
> *me?" and he said to him, "Lord, you know everything; you know that*
> *I love you." Jesus said to him, "Feed my sheep."*

John 21:17

Yes, coaching means correcting, but this should not be the only thing we do. We have to empathize with the spirit of our people and those we steward to know that coaching involves affirming. This requires emotional intelligence because every person is different. We don't want to break the spirit; we want to draw the best out.

In my life, I try to do more inspiring, encouraging, and challenging from a positive perspective. But I also know some need constant direction and therefore turn down the dial of affirmation to a continual need for correction. With these people, I must watch myself and my attitude. And we all have that person we know who has tons of potential but does stupid things all the time. For Jesus, I believe this person was Peter. Peter, his most passionate and impulsive disciple. And guess what? This moment on the beach with Peter after his threefold denial of Christ was perhaps the affirmation Peter needed to get back off the bench and into the spiritual game. From here Peter became one of the great leaders in the first-century church: it was this affirmational moment that launched him.

Speak affirmation to those you lead. For every poke, give a few more pats, and keep drawing the best out of people. They might remember you forever for it, and it could be precisely what they need.

A Coach Addresses Doubt

Jesus immediately reached out his hand and took hold of him, saying to him, "O you of little faith, why did you doubt?"

Matthew 14:31

This again was another consistent practice of Jesus. He was always addressing doubt in his men. This moment of one was perhaps the most famous in the New Testament when Peter had a moment of epic failure in his water walking attempt. But this is what all great coaches do. But notice Jesus does something different.

He does not address his behavior or his initiative, but rather his spiritual issue: doubt. For most followers, this is a prevalent issue that prevents us from spiritual progress; it's disbelief in God. While inspiration and effort come quickly for many of us, we run into the wall of doubt. We doubt because surrounding events convince us they are more real than trust and faith in what God can do, and therefore we need good coaching to help us get back up again. And Jesus here like a great coach, offers a hand (literally) and then allows Peter to troubleshoot the problem, which was his disbelief.

Great spiritual coaches help others address their disbeliefs. We all have them. They are much easier to identify when we have an eye on them as an outside observer. So be on the lookout for opportunities to see someone's disbelief and gently, not forcibly offer a hand and guide them toward great belief in God.

A Coach Intercedes

I [Jesus] do not ask for these only, but also for those who will believe in me through their word, that they may all be one, just as you, Father, are in me, and I in you, that they also may be in us, so that the world may believe that you have sent me.

John 17:20-21

Jesus is caught praying all the time throughout his life. It was a practice he made time for and planned into his daily life. And from how he lived, I assume he was praying all the time, even as he was walking, working, and speaking with others. But there were a few instances in his life where we see him specifically pray for those closest to him. And why does he do this? Well, this is what a great coach does. He prays for those he is allowed to steward. And he does not pray for his benefit but theirs!

This leads to the question that we must ask ourselves, "Are we praying for those we lead and coach?" If not, we shouldand that should change immediately.

A practical way you can incorporate this practice into your life is by posting names (or photos) in places you will commonly see with words or phrases you want to pray over them. For example, I put pictures of those I am praying for on my phone screen saver, or names on my visor in my car so that I see them multiple times each day, and then I am prompted to pray. These visual reminders prompt me time and time again to pray! You can develop your system, but not praying as a coach is *not* an option.

So fellas, get out there and coach today. If it's good enough for Jesus, it's good enough for you.

Reflection & Mentorship

Begin

- Jesus was both a teacher and a coach, and we should be too.

Unpack

- Share about a bad or great coaching experience from your past, without naming the person.
- What made them bad, or what made them great?
- Why has this stuck with you for so long?

Inform

- Choose one of the four texts above.
- What principle do you see in this text?
- Are there additional insights that convict you about this text or interaction of Jesus?

Land

- What concerns do you have about your ability to coach others spiritually?
- What obstacles do you think you are going to have to overcome?
- What one small action can you take as a spiritual coach to those you lead today?

Do

- Take action as a coach by implementing one small behavior into your life this week.

Don't Give Up

There will be times in each of our lives where we feel like the spiritual fire is no longer burning like it once did. As I have worked with men for years, I have discovered that many men will encounter at least one of these moments in his spiritual life. Others of us will have many. They are periods where spiritual fervor is gone, and the fire is not burning like it once used to. And we feel it because the excitement and enthusiasm are noticeably gone. For some, convenience, busyness, and life necessities have quenched the practices and patterns that once fanned the flame of the fire that once burned brightly in our life. While we know this, getting it back is hard work, much like losing the weight we have slowly and steadily put on over the years.

But it's possible to both lose that excess weight, just like it is possible to stoke the fires of our spiritual lives again. And it is for this reason that Paul wrote to the church in Thessalonica. These are his words of encouragement not to give up and keep stoking the fire, and from Paul, we hear three imperatives about how to keep the fire burning.

For you know how, like a father with his children, we exhorted each one of you and encouraged you and charged you to walk in a manner worthy of God, who calls you into his own kingdom and glory.

1 Thessalonians. 2:11-12

Here are Paul's three imperatives for not giving up.

One | Be Exhorted

"We exhorted each one of you..."

We all need to be pressed at times. The word Paul uses here is exhorted. We commonly avoid exhortation for the feelings of shame or guilt it might elicit, but exhortation is necessary. Some of the greatest men I know welcome it and even invite it because they know it will accelerate their growth, character, and fire for the Lord. Exhortation lights the spiritual flame, and often it's the fuel for the flame.

Exhortation means to incite by advice or argument, which means when we are being exhorted, we need correction for a wrong thought, behavior, or motivation. And this has the propensity to sting and stir our insecurities as men. And while many of us don't like it when people tell us the truth through exhortation, sometimes we need to hear the hard truth even though we sometimes cannot handle it. Ouch!

But even so, there were some in Thessalonica who received exhortation from Paul using the gospel truth and, as a result, began to burn with excitement over the new things they were both learning and applying.

Two | Be Courageous

"And encouraged you..."

But it was not only exhortation that Paul administered, but there was an encouragement as well. He took the time to tell them what they were doing wrong and what they were doing right. The fire was lit by exhortation but fanned with the wind of encouragement.

Encouragement gives men courage. Courage to act in faith again and again when we get it right. I know that the occasional correction is essential, but even more, that when we get it right, we should hear that we need to keep repeating this activity. Paul does exactly this. His whole letter to them is multiple chapters of encouragement to press on, keep the faith, and fight the good fight as he continues to hear good reports. And we each need this too as the sparks are relit.

Three | Be Directed

"And charged you to walk in a manner worthy of God."

Finally, he charges them. Paul gives them a mandate in obedience: walk worthy. Notice it's not sprinting or running, it's walking. Slow, systematic, and repetitive down the long road of life. It's as if Paul shouts from afar, "Keep it up, brother!" And we need this too. This is the motivation, inspiration, and the mandate for us all.

But do you know what this all implies?

It implies that you and I both have older and wiser men doing these three things. It assumes we have a man by our side exhorting, encouraging, and directing us. Perhaps if your flame is burning less bright these days, you need these things from a man who can also point you the way so that you as well won't give up. Remember, it's imperative.

Reflection & Mentorship

Begin

- When the spiritual fire is flickering, we may need spiritual exhortation, encouragement, and direction.

Unpack

- How is your spiritual fire today (1-10, low to high)?
- Why is this?

Inform

*For you know how, like a father with his children, we exhorted each
one of you and encouraged you and charged you to walk in a manner
worthy of God, who calls you into his own kingdom and glory.*

1 Thessalonians. 2:11-12

- Identify a few keywords in this text.
- What did Paul intend to communicate?

Land

- Of the three points above, which one do you need right
  now to light the spiritual fire in your life?
- What might prevent you from getting this?
- What could be done today about this?

Do

- Ensure you have an older wiser man speaking truth into
  your life. And ask him some good questions this week.

Be Teachable & Coachable

In life, a teachable spirit is an essential attribute of manhood. Our teachability quotient is the determining factor for us to become better men, employees, athletes, and leaders. And even when we "arrive" at a place of high proficiency through education or expertise, we never transcend the need to have a teachable spirit.

Followership assumes that we are a perpetual student. As a fallen man, we understand that based on what we read in the bible, we are continually sinful, and all our intentions are evil, that no one is righteous, and thus we fall short of God's glory.

The Lord saw that the wickedness of man was great in the earth,
and that every intention of the thoughts of his heart was only evil
continually.

Genesis 6:5

None is righteous, no, not one.

Romans 3:10

For all have sinned and fall short of the glory of God.

Romans 3:23

Thus the need for Christ. It was he who showed us the way to life and godliness. And as men who claim him as our Savior, we commit to a life of followership that assumes we must be taught a new way: *The* Way. Therefore it is us who must be trained, and thus daily, we need a teachable spirit, for this makes for great athletes in the same way it makes for great men of God.

Be teachable, not stupid.

Whoever loves discipline loves knowledge,
but he who hates reproof is stupid.

Proverbs 12:1

There are different types of discipline here. One is a self-inflicted discipline; this is the type that we choose to subject our character, behavior, and desires, too, because we know that it will produce positive results. The other is an others-inflicted discipline called here "reproof," and this is executed on us by others because we are not able to inflict discipline ourselves. They are both painful, and they both have the potential to produce positive results. That is unless we hate it; then we are stupid.

Too frequently, I believe we men only learn from others-inflicted pain. This should not be the case. As men, we should, with a teachable proactive spirit, seek to be taught and self-inflict the discipline. We do this in other instances, but rarely when it comes to our faith. We need to be a little more proactive, and we are when we are teachable.

Receive instruction and increase.

Give instruction to a wise man, and he will be still wiser; teach a
righteous man, and he will increase in learning.

Proverbs 9:9

You know a few of these people. They are men who are always aggressively maturing in wisdom, knowledge, and understanding. They seek wisdom. They crave understanding. They desire knowledge. They will dig up a field looking for its riches. Their determination and drive are inspiring. And they don't do it to learn they do it to grow closer to Christ, increase intimacy with him, and because they desire righteousness.

I always thought as I got older that I would naturally become less sinful. This former assumption is now proved wrong in my life. I realize today that I was sinful, but now I am called righteous, yet at the same time, I am also becoming increasingly aware of the depth, impact, and ramifications of my sin. I would say that while I am growing wiser with it, my awareness is growing, and thus my need for more of God's truth when God's truth is needed more than ever before.

Do you want to be wise? The answer is simple; receive God's "instruction and be wiser still."

Reflection & Mentorship

Begin

- Great followers are always teachable.

Unpack

- Are men in general teachable? Why or why not?
- What is your level of teachability? (1-10, low to high)

Inform

Whoever loves discipline loves knowledge,
but he who hates reproof is stupid.

Proverbs 12:1

Give instruction to a wise man, and he will be still wiser;
teach a righteous man, and he will increase in learning.

Proverbs 9:9

- Which verse do you more need to hear today? Explain why?

Land

- What is convicting to you right now about your level of teachability?
- What would level this up one degree?
- What one step do you need to take?
- What one obstacle do you think you might face when trying to take this step?

Do

- Take that step above and make sure you do it today.

The Benefits of Practice

There are a lot of sports I love to play. One I love to play (but don't practice enough) is golf. And I have learned over the years if I want to get better I am going to have to practiceand I mean practice a lot! For me, this would mean a significant investment of time, energy, and money, and I am not too sure I have enough of any of those three things to make me that much better than I am now because of all the bad habits I have developed over the years.

But spiritual practice is not a nice idea; it's a requirement. We must do it. For when we do it increases three things in our life

Increased Application

> *What you have learned and received and heard and seen in me practice these things, and the God of peace will be with you.*

Philippians 4:9

There are somethings we learn by watching the lives of others. Paul, as a keen and prolific teacher, understood this factor in spiritual practice. Some of our practices are a little hard to know unless we watch or listen to someone do it. For example, prayer is a practice about which volumes of books have been written., but still, even the disciples wanted Jesus to show them how to pray. And much of the time, Jesus prayed out loud so they could see and hear how a prayer looks and sounds.

We, too, must apply the disciplines to understand how to practice them more effectively. For example, I have learned a lot more about giving financially to my church by practicing it. I have learned a lot more from reading the Bible on my own than listening to someone teach about it. I have learned more from serving, teaching, and training in my family than considering what it might look like to do it. We should watch what others godly men do, but we must also put it into practice and do it to discover a new dimension of spiritual application.

Increased Skill

But they who wait for the Lord shall renew their strength; they shall mount up with wings like eagles; they shall run and not be weary; they shall walk and not faint.

Isaiah 40:31

Practicing may mean to develops skills in those "non-active" exercises, Waiting, as the writer references here, is a something we all need practice with. But notice the art and skill of practicing the discipline of waiting on the Lord leads to a benefit: renewed strength. It might seem a little counterintuitive, but it's not.

Those non-active exercises develop great virtue in men. Things like waiting, patience, withholding vengeance, moderating anger, speaking kindly, and loving those who hate us require self-control. At times, we must say "no" to the self, which is challenging for men.

Increased Clarity

But be doers of the word, and not hearers only, deceiving yourselves.

James 1:22

There is a big difference between hearing alone and then hearing combined with doing what God says. The New Testament had a word for this: hypocrisy. To be a hypocrite is to be a pretender, a faker, an actor, but not a Christian. Jesus spoke challenging messages to those who lived hypocritical lives because of how poorly it witnessed others about who God was. And James challenges us to do the same.

Doing what we read in Scripture is more challenging than we sometimes realize because action requires effort and change. We, men, love to be challenged, inspired, and motivatedbut taking action is something only we can do as individuals. Yet I have learned that if I immediately take action, I am blessed in the doing. I encourage men to apply quickly and act on the convictions and prompting of the Holy Spirit. While our activity is never going to be perfect, it is better than doing nothing, for in doing something we learn. And sometimes we discover another way not to do something, but that's okay, right? For example, Peter did fail at walking on water, but on the other hand, he is one of the only men in all of history to walk on water (besides Jesus) because he acted by getting out of the boat. So, do it promptly.

Reflection & Mentorship

Begin

- Practice has benefits: application, skill, and clarity.

Unpack

- Are men good at practicing what they are being taught in God's Word?
- What evidence do you have for your position?
- Is this more a matter of ineffective teaching and discipleship, or is it a problem with weak action and application?

Inform

- Of the three scriptures above, which was the most convicting for you?
- Explain why?

Land

- What one thing do you need to put into practice this week?
- Who is someone you could go to get wisdom on how to do this more effectively?
- What question do you want to ask him?

Do

- Have a meeting with the man you mentioned above this week.

Endurance Wins

Too many Christians today lack endurance. During times of excess, we tend to grow fat and lazy in our spiritual lives and quickly forget the suffering that the fathers of the faith endured for our sake. Endurance is the Christian commitment that all men need in the face of persecution and difficulty. All men need it and should invite it into their spiritual lives.

Endurance Produces

More than that, we rejoice in our sufferings, knowing that suffering produces endurance, and endurance produces character, and character produces hope.

Romans 5:3-4

Those who compete know the value of endurance. While the physical suffering of training is hard, those that have faced it time and time again see that right on the other side of pain are the benefits of endurance, character, and hope. But those who quit before realizing this miss out on seeing the profound benefits.

Endurance assumes that we will spiritually challenge ourselves and push beyond what is a comfortable limit. And if you feel like you have been too comfortable or perhaps you've plateaued, then maybe suffering would produce what you need to give you that life for the stage and phase of your life.

For example, consider the activity of resistance training. Why do we do this? We do this to push our muscles beyond what they usually can bear, which results in the tearing of the muscle tissue so the muscle will grow. While sweating, pressing, straining, and tearing can at times be painful, it results in growth and increased strength over time, and this is the same in our spiritual life except it is strength and hope in Christ we are building. So never underestimate the benefit of endurance in your life and pushing through the challenges with God.

Endurance in God's Will

For you have need of endurance, so that when you have done the will of God you may receive what is promised.

Hebrews 10:36

God's sovereign will must come to pass. And in a battle of wills with God, we will always lose. But guess what our loss may also be our win!

We are all in a battle with God's will all the time; we may not recognize it. Our will and his will are continually doing battle about our purpose, possessions, and position on politics. And while the self is driven to want more of it and have our way, God reminds us that he is Lord of all things, even our life. And we, as the subject and slave of Christ, need this reminder. We are called followers, after all, and the person we are following is God.

Daily I must submit my will to his will even though it is a constant wrestling match. But the good part is when I lose, I also win. Our mandate is this—do the will of God and receive the promise.

At the End of Endurance is a Crown

Blessed is the man who remains steadfast under trial, for when he has stood the test, he will receive the crown of life, which God has promised to those who love him.

James 1:12

Sometimes endurance is not only developed by pushing through suffering by taking action but also my only remaining steadfast and immovable in character and faith during the trial. For example, when a marathon runner hits mile 20 and must push through the pain, here his muscles might be fit, but his mind needs to tell his muscles to keep moving forward. More often than not, this is what endurance looks like for a Christian in a long trial. For example, a lengthy trial with a wayward child, a personal physical illness, or an ongoing tragedy in a family's life.

Either way, the promise here is "the crown of life," and I love that the writer James draws our attention to the prize at the end. This is critical for those enduring the lengthy trials, for we must keep our eyes fixed on the prize at the end and focus a little less on the present suffering.

Reflection & Mentorship

Begin

- Endurance produces benefit in God's will and promises a crown.

Unpack

- Can you think of a biblical example of endurance?
- What does this example teach us about endurance?
- Is this lesson easy or hard to learn? Why?

Inform

- Of the three texts above, which one is the hardest for most men to apply? Why is this so?

Land

- Where in your life, do you need endurance? Perhaps name the suffering your enduring.
- What needs to happen for you to have more endurance in this area?

Do

- Take action by finding a brother to pray for your endurance as a man of God.

The Ironman

It is a hard-won designation: Ironman. It is one of the premier examples of endurance and perseverance. It takes work, grit, discipline, and resolve to complete that race.

Jesus demonstrated that kind of resolve and perseverance in his ministry. He is the premier example of the resolute man. Notice the next verse; it contains the only appearance of the word resolute in the entire Bible.

As the time approached for him to be taken up to heaven, Jesus resolutely set out for Jerusalem.

Luke 9:51

This moment was a significant turning point in Christ's ministry. Up until this point, Jesus was insistent with his disciples that they be quiet about his identity and his mission. But now, in Luke 9:51 there is a definitive change, as if his life's final race is to be run. And the word chosen to describe this turn is "resolute." As we continue to read the narrative of his ministry, we watch his resolve and charge get sharper and more evident as he makes his way to the cross. I believe this word describes not only who Jesus is but who most men want to be: resolute men who live all-in men for Jesus Christ.

But fellas, this is who I want to be. I want to have that same resolute determination living all-in the way that Jesus lived: going the distance, determined, desisting the ways of my past, directed by God, living with discipline for completing the race God has given me.

What does that race look like for us?

While we are each different and the races we run have different paths, there are some constants in becoming resolute and living all-in for Jesus.

First | We run knowing our life belongs to the Lord.

> *For if we live, we live to the Lord, and if we die, we die to the Lord.*
> *So then, whether we live or whether we die, we are the Lord's.*

Romans 14:8

Anyone competing in the Ironman knows that his life belongs to the race. This race is their life and their identity, and once you finish, you receive the designation. As we run with Jesus, we know that we have already won the race because Christ ran it for usbut yet we run as we have already won. And why? Because by nature of his title Lord we have our titlesubject, servant, and slave of Jesus Christ. While the race is run and the title is designated, we still run in a way that represents him. And as Paul says, "We live to Lord" or "We die to the Lord" because everything is about him, and nothing can get in the way of completing that race. If our lives belong to him, we see every day as a training session that will help us complete the race God has given us.

Second | We will fail, but we find strength in God.

> *My flesh and my heart may fail, but God is the strength of my heart*
> *and my portion forever.*

Psalm 73:26

Yes, you are going to fail. Sorry, that's the bad news. But the good news is the strength to go on does not come from you. It's not about you finding the strength to get back up again. It's God who will give you the power you need in those moments you fail, so you will discover that it is his strength you need, not yours. And these moments are vital since we need to run the race and finish the race.

But the great thing about failure in our competition is that we learn to discipline the desires and the motivation in the process of running. And this is important because in our race, how we run is more important. After all, it has already been won. The crown is ours. All we have to do is continuing running and learn how to let the Lord be the Lord.

And thus fellas, we practice here. Our lives are training for the final race. And the more we practice and fail, the more we learn. As we allow the Holy Spirit to convict and the Lord to lead, we will look back and realize that we are becoming a more faith-filled disciple. When you fail, learn, dust yourself off, and keep moving forward, resolutely in God's strength.

Third | Be a finisher not just a starter

I have finished the race, I have kept the faith.

2 Timothy 4:7

No one who competes in the Ironman would tell you that it is easy. Even the best of athletes. It can be excruciating. But anyone who finishes has the satisfaction that they did itthey completed the race!

Just before Jesus breathed his last breath on the cross, he exclaimed, "It is finished." These words capture the call of this resolute and all-in man. He was not just a starter but a finisher. He recognized the end but saw it from the start. And this is what resolute men do. When they start, they understand that there is an end, and they run with this marker in mind.

Are you with me? Are you resolute? Are you ready to live all-in?

Reflection & Mentorship

Begin

- We run a resolute race as men who live all-in for Christ.

Unpack

- Have you ever competed in an endurance event? What is the process like?
- What transferrable concepts are there in endurance training to running the spiritual race?

Inform

- There are three texts above, which one is the one you needed to hear today?
- Why is this important to men as we live the Christian life and run our individual races?

Land

- What one thing do you need to run more resolutely?
- Who is someone you look to who might show you how to develop in this area?

Do

- Reach out to this person today.

The Man in The Arena

"It is not the critic who counts; not the man who points out
how the strong man stumbles, or where the doer of deeds
could have done them better. The credit belongs to the man
who is actually in the arena, whose face is marred by dust
and sweat and blood; who strives valiantly; who errs, who
comes short again and again, because there is no effort
without error and shortcoming; but who does actually strive
to do the deeds; who knows great enthusiasms, the great
devotions; who spends himself in a worthy cause; who at the
best knows in the end the triumph of high achievement, and
who at the worst, if he fails, at least fails while daring greatly,
so that his place shall never be with those cold and timid
souls who neither know victory nor defeat."

THEODORE ROOSEVELT.

What a quote. Perhaps one of the great ones for men today.

God upholds the man in the arena.

This is a pretty good picture of the life we men live in Christ.

We fail all the time: words we wish we could take back; reactions we want to
do over; marriages we wish we could have saved; decisions that were foolish
and got us into trouble; or just the circumstances of life that dealt us a bad

hand. But gentlemen, fallen people do fallen things, and a fallen world delivers fallen conditions. But God is always present, always redeems and is still waiting for us to trust Him, get back up dust off, wipe off the sweat and blood, and get back into the game.

Though he fall, he shall not be cast headlong,
for the Lord upholds his hand.

Psalm 37:24

These are great words to us fallen men, and I am sure President Roosevelt knew these words. They are firm to beaten up and defeated men. It is God who reaches down to his man, offers a firm hand, and lifts him. And this man is you the man in the arena.

Jesus is with the man in the arena.

The writer of Hebrews says this about Jesus.

Since then we have a great high priest who has passed through the heavens, Jesus, the Son of God, let us hold fast our confession. For we do not have a high priest who is unable to sympathize with our weaknesses, but one who in every respect has been tempted as we are, yet without sin. Let us then with confidence draw near to the throne of grace, that we may receive mercy and find grace to help in time of need.

Hebrews 4:14-16

This is an excellent reminder to men who are on the field of battle. It's by *mercy* and *grace* that we find help when we feel beaten in the arena of life. But the additional detail we cannot miss is that Jesus has been in the arena with us. He does not sympathize with the battle from afar, but he empathizes with us because he is in it. And the grace and mercy that sustains us are the same that sustained him.

I am comforted in knowing that as I fight my battles, and you yours, we are battling and beaten by the same challenges Christ faced. We are not alone. Please hear me: you are not alone! We are in this together with him. Therefore be confident in him.

Are you even in the arena?

Join me. Christ in the fight of your life. It will leave you bloodied and broken, but you are not alone. Don't let others or your past keep you from the greatest experience of your life. God is there. Christ is with you. Get in the arena and join the battle. Become the man that God wants you to be for him. And get off the bench and into the spiritual battle. It will refine you, shape you, and define you as a man of God.

Reflection & Mentorship

Begin

- Be a man in the arena with God upholding and Christ by your side.

Unpack

- Are Christian men joining the battle in the arena?
- What is the battle in the arena about during our time?
- Do you feel like you are in the arena?

Inform

- The two texts above highlight God and Jesus and how they aid a man during battle. What did you learn from these two texts?
- Or what words stood out to you from these two scriptures?

Land

- Are you in the arena?
- If so, how does it feel?
- If not, how are you going to get into the arena?
- What help do you need in the arena?
- What one step can you take to get that help?

Do

- Get help, call, text, or meet with someone for biblical wisdom today.

Coached for Courage

ike many men, I've watched the movies like *Braveheart, Gladiator, Rocky,* and others too many times. I think men are drawn to these stories because we see in them something we want to see in ourselves. In the present culture, where men are increasingly enduring distress and oppression for both being a man, following Christ, and believing in the Bible's truth, we are discovering that courage is a necessary virtue that must be lived out in new ways.

For example, we are drawn to the courage of William Wallace, who battles unthinkable odds in a revolt against the King of England, whose troops had pillaged, raped, and killed his people, including his bride. William's causefreedom from oppression and injusticewas something he was willing to die for even if it cost him his life. Today men must rediscover courage, and though the causes do not changestanding for justice against injusticewe must live it out in new ways.

Take, for example, Joshua, who was Moses's successor. God's words to Joshua have echoed down through time from one generation of believers to the next.

> *Be strong and courageous, for you shall cause this people to inherit the land that I swore to their fathers to give them. Only be strong and very courageous, being careful to do according to all the law that Moses my servant commanded you. Do not turn from it to the right hand or to the left, that you may have good success wherever*

you go. This Book of the Law shall not depart from your mouth, but you shall meditate on it day and night, so that you may be careful to do according to all that is written in it. For then you will make your way prosperous, and then you will have good success. Have I not commanded you? Be strong and courageous. Do not be frightened, and do not be dismayed, for the Lord your God is with you wherever you go.

Joshua 1:6-9

Joshua was known for his courage. Before this moment, he was one of the twelve spies that Moses had sent in to spy out the land forty years earlier. Only Joshua and Caleb of the twelve had recommended following the command of God to take the land. The other ten men convinced the people that it was too dangerous, and because of their reported fear, the people disobeyed God. For Joshua, the answer was simple. Have courage and faith, and God will ensure our success. And of course, because of their fear, only Joshua and Caleb would enter the promised land many years later.

But now Joshua receives the leadership baton from Moses as he inherits the call to lead the people of God. God instructs Joshua to do one thing, and that's to have the courage to trust in Him. That's it. Nothing more. And thus, we have a definition of courage. Courage is trust in God in the face of human uncertainty.

But for years, God had been preparing Joshua as he developed his courage in many smaller moments, like the moment with the 12 spies. And doesn't this make you ask yourself if perhaps God has been coaching you as well to have courage?

We encounter small moments of courage all the time. When we open up our life to other men. When we get honest about our sin. When we face into a repetitive sin challenge. When we take the spiritual lead at home. When we seek forgiveness. When we stand up for injustice. When we love those who hate us. When we return good for evil. When we pray for those who persecute us. Each of these moments builds courage in a man's life to coach him for moments that will require even greater courage.

When Jesus says, "Follow me," he is calling us to a courageous coaching adventure. It's courageous to live his life, one often opposed to the values and virtue of the world. But we take him at his word and follow his commands knowing that he too will be with us wherever we go. As men of God, there an area in your life today where God has been talking to you, and you need the courage to say, "I will do it?"

Reflection & Mentorship

Begin

- Jesus is willing to coach us in courage if we are willing to follow him.

Unpack

- Rate your courage quotient from 1-10 (low to high).
- Why did you give yourself this rating?

Inform

Be strong and courageous, for you shall cause this people to inherit the land that I swore to their fathers to give them. Only be strong and very courageous, being careful to do according to all the law that Moses my servant commanded you. Do not turn from it to the right hand or to the left, that you may have good success wherever you go. This Book of the Law shall not depart from your mouth, but you shall meditate on it day and night, so that you may be careful to do according to all that is written in it. For then you will make your way prosperous, and then you will have good success. Have I not

commanded you? Be strong and courageous. Do not be frightened,
and do not be dismayed, for the Lord your God is with you
wherever you go.

Joshua 1:6-9

- What observations do you make about this text?
- What message was God trying to convey to Joshua?
- What does this mean to us today?

Land

- What area of your life do you need coaching in courage right now?
- What specific wisdom do you need?
- Who is someone who could help?
- How does this text speak to that issue?
- What one thing could you do today to be more courageous?

Do

- Take action—be courageous.

Workout Partner

A man of many companions may come to ruin, but there is a
friend who sticks closer than a brother.

PROVERBS 18:24

I don't know about you, but when I work out with a partner, I work out
harder. There's something essential about this. I know when I lay down on
the bench press without a partner, I am a little more hesitant and don't
push as farbecause I don't have a spotter. But when I have a spotter, I am
willing to push harder and heavier weight because I got someone watching
out for me, encouraging me, and pushing me.

I think this is applicable to our spiritual life. We need a workout partner.
We need someone who will watch out for us and push us spiritually.
Unfortunately, many men don't have a partner. We think we can get by
without a spotter, but then life gets too heavy, and sin gets too weighty, and
there we stand all alone with the weight of the world on our chest and no
one to help lift it off.

But I know most men want a spiritual spotter, partner, buddy, and friend. We
don't always know how to identify what we are looking for in brotherhood,
and therefore we don't ask. Many of us have never experienced it before,
so we don't know what it should look like. What does a spiritual brother
spotter look like? And who would be best for us and in our journey of
becoming men of God?

Here are three marks of a great spiritual brother.

Mark One | Acceptance and Encouragement

We long for relationships, yes, with women, but we also need relationships with men. And we need to have some spiritual men in our lives. We need brothers or, at minimum, a brother who will both accept and encourage us. They will be men who want the best for us despite our hurts and hang-ups. These should be men who know how to extend us love, grace, mercy, and forgiveness. And they are men who we can do the same.

I think both acceptance and encouragement from these men are important: acceptance when we fail and encouragement that keeps us moving. Like a spotter, they know when and where we are likely to fail and can almost anticipate it. And when we drop the bar or push the limits, they are there to help us back up or cheering us to push a little harder.

I know it may be harder than we think to find this person, but they are out there.

Mark Two | Grace and Truth

Another mark of a great brother is their willingness to speak both grace and truth. Unconditional acceptance, coupled with the desire, to be honest, is what all great friends do. We don't need men barking at us all the time being legalistic about everything we do—this is constricting and leads exhaustion. On the other hand, we don't want a good friend to lie to us when we might be headed for disaster around the next bend.

Just as Jesus came to us full of grace and truth, we extend grace to each other and be willing to speak truth to each other. Grace without truth will not help us grow while truth without grace is hard and judgmental.

Mark Three | Safe and Healthy

We need brothers to whom we can reveal our true selves and struggles without fear of abandonment. This is healthy in that we don't stay the way we are, but allow key people to speak into our lives so that we become betterand we extend the same grace and truth to them. This combination is a rare gift to any relationship.

I have found these attributes mark some of my best relationships with men. Look for men who exhibit these marks, and you will walk away from your interactions encouraged rather than discouraged. Also, think about how you can give the gift of this kind of brotherhood to others. The more we focus on being the kind of friend that Jesus is, the more significant our influence on others will be.

Reflection & Mentorship

Begin

- We all need a spiritual workout partner who is helps us become a better man.

Unpack

- What are the attributes of a work partner you would seek in another man?

Inform

A man of many companions may come to ruin, but there is a friend who sticks closer than a brother.

Proverbs 18:24

- What does this verse mean?
- Do you have a close friend? What is his name?
- Why is he a "close" friend to you?

Land

- Choose to discuss one of the following:
- What are you looking for in a spiritual brother?
- What could you do to take your relationship with your current spiritual brother to another level spiritually?

Do

- Take action on the above; either build a spiritual relationship or expand a current relationship spiritually.

Never Give Up

I cannot count how many times I have been in the middle of some high-intensity workout that I wanted to quit. It has happened to me on many occasions. As I have listened carefully to my body I have discovered a few reasons. First, my mind is not in it because I am distracted by other things. Second, my body is overworked or overtired from a previous workout or not enough sleep. Third, I have not eaten well throughout the day; therefore, by the time I reach the workout I am already low on energy. And when these three factors come together in combination, at best, my workout is an "active recovery" day.

But I do, on occasion, have those days I feel like I can conquer anything. For some reason my mind is willing to push through the wall; my body is rested; and my food energy is just right. In these moments, I have felt invincible! Then look back to see a lot of others falling behindand because I am a little competitive at timesI would say this feels pretty good, if not very good!

But we know not every day is like this. We all know that the days we feel great are far outnumbered by the days we do not. And this means on the days we don't that we must not give up since there is far more to learn in the days we are not performing at our best than the ones we do. And it is in light of this that Paul the apostle reminds the church in Galatia with these words.

And let us not grow weary of doing good, for in due season we will reap, if we do not give up.

Galatians 6:9

Here are a few things Paul is trying to communicate to them about a timeless axiom of the faith: never give up.

One | You are going to get tired.

This is a reality. But for some reason, we don't think it is going to happen to us as Christians. But it happens in our workouts, just like it happens when we exercise our faith. There are days you won't want to act like a Christian. Maybe because you have "other" things on your mind. Maybe because you are spiritually exhausted. Maybe the input of your spiritual disciplines is low. In any event, it happens! And the feeling at this moment is much like those moments you hit the wall in a workout. You know what happens? You want to stop and go home.

Paul does not deny this. He knows the Galatians are tired. Tired of the stress that their faith generated from the opposition around them. With this opposition came resistance, and bearing up under this resistance was making some weary. But we must remember weariness will come. And therefore, when it strikes, we must not back off or back down. These are the moments we must endure in the faith for the benefit of our ongoing development.

And how do we respond?

Two | Do good when you feel weary.

I think Paul's point is well taken. When we get tired, we get lazy, and then we don't act like faithful men. I don't know about you, but when I get spiritually tired, my mindset changes, my attitude changes, and my responses change. But Paul says instead, *"do good,"* and he's right because this is precisely what is most needed.

God does great things with us in those moments that we don't feel like doing good things for him. By doing good even when I don't like it, I discover how to push through that ominous, ever-talked about "wall" that we all eventually hit. But more often than not, the benefit is for me more than in the good I do for others.

This means we cannot be spiritually lazy. When the mindset sours, the attitude changes, and the spiritual self-discipline is fading these are the moments to lean in a little more. Doing good, even when we don't feel like, is a good thing. But until you do it, you will not discover the benefits.

And this brings us to the benefit.

Three | Reap the benefits of not giving up.

I believe so many Christians want the benefits without putting in the work. And here's why, they assume salvation, while free, assumes spiritual laziness and abuses the benefits of God's grace.

> *Well then, since God's grace has set us free from the law, does that*
> *mean we can go on sinning? Of course not!*

Romans 6:15

In our spiritual journey, we reap benefits now and then, and this should inspire us. While we are driven by God's grace now, we must keep an eye on the unseen benefits then. Therefore we must "go to work" and "reap" these benefits. And thus, Paul assumes we are going to act.

Go to work in your faith. Live as a man who is redeemed but yet at the same work as one approved with one eye on the benefits at the end, and the benefits for you along the way. And work hard. Work with all your might, not because you have earned anything yourself, but because Christ worked hard for you and your benefit.

Let's follow in the Savior's shoes and do good when you feel weary, reap the benefits, and never give up.

Reflection & Mentorship

Begin

- We must never give up on doing good.

Unpack

- Have Christians become lazy? Share why or why not.
- Do we also easily give up? Share why or why not.

Inform

*And let us not grow weary of doing good, for in due season
we will reap, if we do not give up.*

Galatians 6:9

- How is this a loving charge by the apostle Paul?
- How do you think the Galatians received it?
- Would this inspire you?

Land

- Is there a place in your life you have become tired or lazy?
- Can you identify why you feel tired or perhaps lazy?
- What one small thing can you do today to do good?

Do

- Do one good action today. Do not be weary. Reap the benefits.

The Man of Great Strength

When we think of men of great strength in the Bible, the first to come to mind is Samson. He was a man upon whom God gave the blessing of physical strength to deliver his people, but as we know he life was not as heroic as you would think it would be. Given superhuman ability, he squandered and misused it, but still, we learn great lessons from Samson on how to be a man of great strength. Here are a few that I have found insightful that I believe will inspire you to be strong in the Lord.

Lesson One | It takes strength to associate with godly people.

Samson went down to Timnah, and at Timnah he saw one of the daughters of the Philistines. 2 Then he came up and told his father and mother, "I saw one of the daughters of the Philistines at Timnah. Now get her for me as my wife."

Judges 14:1-2

It may be hard to see from this quick read of this text, but the people who were oppressing Israel were the Philistines. They were the enemy of Israel and Samson. Yet he chose not to only associate with them; he decided to marry into them, which was forbidden by the vow he took before God.

As we associate with the wrong people, the wrong truth, the wrong advice, and the wrong lifestyle, we eventually become like the wrong people. We need to remember that in this short life we steward we need the right people, the right truth, the right advice, and the right lifestyle to become the right people. And yes, we should influence others along the way, but we find godly strength in godly associations. Here is Christ's charge:

And he said to all, "If anyone would come after me, let him deny himself and take up his cross daily and follow me."

Luke 9:23

If anyone comes to me and does not hate his own father and mother and wife and children and brothers and sisters, yes, and even his own life, he cannot be my disciple.

Luke 14:26

Jesus demanded both association and disassociation, and there is strength found in doing so because when we follow him, we are stronger together.

And though a man might prevail against one who is alone, two will withstand him

a threefold cord is not quickly broken.

Ecclesiastes 4:12

Lesson Two | It takes strength to act and give glory to God.

And Samson said, "With the jawbone of a donkey, heaps upon heaps, with the jawbone of a donkey have I struck down a thousand men."

Judges 15:16

Even though Samson had moments of great, God-given physical strength unfortunately we see little glory given to the God who gave him this strength. His feats of strength missed the opportunity to act out on God's mission, purpose, and vision for his life. Most of the time, we see Samson's exhibiting strength only to avenge his loss, and while God continued to fulfill his promise of strength to him, Samson continues to use his power for the wrathful vengeance and self-glory.

While we can be easily amazed at what Samson did here with a jawbone of an ass, how much more glorious would this have been if he had done it for the right reason, in the right way, and at the finish gave the right person the glory!

Being strong in Christ means diverting attention away from us and toward God. While we are given gifts, and many of these are magnificent, we need to remember that all things come from God alone: our skills, talents, and abilities are all his, we are merely stewards of these and when they accomplish great things, we must remember to give glory to him and not "steal" it for ourselves.

Lesson Three | It takes strength to stay far from disobedience.

So Delilah said to Samson, "Please tell me where your great strength lies, and how you might be bound, that one could subdue you."

Judges 16:6

This part of Samson's story is perhaps the most infamous. With Delilah, he has finally met the match of his superhuman strength. After a lot of coercion, he gives in to her ploys to uncovering the secret to his great strength, and finally, he is detained and captured.

This part of the story is disappointing for me as a man reading the narrative of his life. The lesson is great: men of renowned strength stay far from sin, and the things or people that will tempt them to sin. Samson's weakness was a beautiful woman, and you think he would have known that by this point in his life. But in his arrogance, he thought he could walk the line, and in the adventure of these moments kept getting closer and closer to sin. Instead, he should have run further and further, which is what strong men do. Strong men know their weaknesses and flee at the hint of immorality.

Men, we have been given great strength. The very power of God dwells within us. Go today in his strength, and give him glory in all you do.

Reflection & Mentorship

Begin

- Men of great strength, associate with the right people, give glory to the right person, and stay away from the wrong behaviors.

Unpack

- Which superhuman power do you wish you had?
- Is it hard to believe Samson had superhuman strength?
- Who is a modern athlete who has what appears to be a superhuman ability?

Inform

- Why is the story of Samson so important for men?
- Which of the three points above convicted you?

Land

- What item or issue do you need to give attention to today?
- How would your life be different if you did?

Do

- Discover your superhuman power this week by doing one of the following all week:
- Leaning on a Christian brother for help.
- Giving glory to God when you do something well.
- Fleeing disobedience when sin awaits.

The Dangers of Success

Pride goes before destruction,
and a haughty spirit before a fall.

PROVERBS 16:18

We all love success. Some of us will chase it and never find it. Others will find it and discover the challenge of it. This could happen on the sporting field or in the game of life, but as it occurs we need to be wary of the hidden dangers that accompany victory and success. Like you, I have watched as many great leaders burn out and fail when their success becomes a burden to their ability to continue moving forward. And for some men success will become intoxicating. They will drink of success and grow increasingly drunk on the feeling, only to experience a tragic fall from glory, which is usually sudden and publicly embarrassing at the same time.

Here are three valuable lessons to remember in our victory or the next time we experience success.

One | Don't believe your own press

With success comes greater confidence and proficiency, which is usually an excellent thing. However, self-confidence has a shadow side that might lie to us, saying, "You killed it, and you did this all on your own." These thoughts are persuasive, private, and powerful. They frequently come back and bite us.

While our competencies in life should and will grow, we must remember that God and others have also made us the men we are today. Everything we have learned we have learned from someone else. We discover nothing on our own for all things that are revealed only and always by God.

> *Not that we are sufficient in ourselves to claim anything as coming from us, but our sufficiency is from God.*
>
> 2 Corinthians 3:5

When we experience success, we need to preach verses like this to ourselves, reminding ourselves that it is not our press we seek; it is God's. As followers, we give up our right to seek our glory: we are subject and servant only to him. It is him we serve and worship. We pray, give, sing to *him*, not *self*. And in every success, God gets all the glory, which reminds us not to seek our own. Continuing down a path of self-praise will only lead to narcissism, which results in a great fall.

Two | Don't marginalize the godly voices

Have you ever worked for someone who didn't listen to people who disagreed with them, but cultivated those who did? We all have. Why does this happen? Because some leaders have become so successfulconfident of their own abilitythat they ignore the insights of those around them, especially those with contrarian positions. This happens in businesses and churches alike.

Just consider this moment where Rehoboam made a decisive decision that led to the destruction of the kingdom.

But he abandoned the counsel that the old men gave him and took
counsel with the young men who had grown up with him
and stood before him.

1 Kings 12:8

Long term successful men and leaders always want a variety of voices around them. They even invite challenges because they know it makes them and others better. But this does not mean they act out on every opinion that comes their way, but they are definitely willing to consider and weight the thoughts and ideas of others respectfully. Especially those that challenge them and those who are wiser than they. Unhealthy leaders don't want to hear from those who challenge because they have started to believe that they are usually if not always right. The more successful we are the more likely we are to marginalize those who disagree with us, which places us in significant danger.

Third | Don't isolate

Eventually, success can lead to isolation. This happens because success drives us to find a retreat from the public eye or perhaps the attention that success has broughtfame. But isolation can be a very bad thing.

In the spring of the year, the time when kings go out to battle, David
sent Joab, and his servants with him, and all Israel.
And they ravaged the Ammonites and besieged Rabbah.
But David remained at Jerusalem.

2 Samuel 11:1

Many of us know that King David's choice to stay home from war is precisely what led to his notorious sin with Bathsheba. While success can cause us to isolate, there is a type of isolation that is not good for any man.

In isolation from work, brothers, accountability stemming from success, we might inadvertently leave a door open to sin. And why? Because all the good things we once did, we can no longer do like we did, therefore we isolate only to find nothing but the opportunity for sin, which becomes our undoing.

In isolation we are open to failure. We are not accountable and don't allow others to speak into our lives. In these moments we remove the guardrails of our lives, leaving us open and vulnerable to our proclivities, our narcissism, and we are no longer listening to those who want to help us make the best decisions.

This is the ultimate danger of success when we don't put adequate guard rails around our lives. Isolation leads to a disaster at some point. Those who have experienced failure after significant success can often point back to a time when they quit listening to those who challenged them, decided that the rules didn't apply to them, and always made the right calls. It might be moral, financial, relational, or some other type of failure, but often reputation is lost as is the fruit of their hard work.

Here is the lesson: the greater our success, the greater our potential for failure unless we resist the temptation to believe our press. We must listen to those who tell us the truth, stay connected in real genuine relationships, and keep guardrails in our lives.

> *Trust in the Lord with all your heart,*
> *and do not lean on your own understanding.*
> *In all your ways acknowledge him,*
> *and he will make straight your paths.*

Proverbs 3:5-6

Reflection & Mentorship

Begin

- There are dangers in success, so don't believe your own press; don't marginalize and don't isolate.

Unpack

- Who is someone you know who had a great fall from great success?
- What was the reason for their fall?

Inform

- Of the three texts above, which one convicted you?
- What action is God calling you to make as a result of reading this?

Land

- Are you in danger of a fall at present?
- What issue do you need to address in your life today?

Do

- Take one prevented action today to avert your fall from success in your life.